Presents:

how to start a small business on a tight budget: the checklist

Rada A. Machin, Esq.
Partner, Owner
The Machin Law Firm, LLC

DEDICATION

I dedicate this book to my business partner and great love Manny. Thanks
for dreaming with me.
A special thanks to my Mom and Dad, for believing in me, always.
I love you all.

LEGAL DISCLAIMER

This is a consumer guide book. This book is not intended to give legal advice. It is meant for educational purposes only. For specific legal advice, consult an attorney with business law experience. If you wish to consult with Mrs. Machin about a specific case, her contact information is below.

The Machin Law Firm, LLC
info@machinlawfirm.com
www.machinlawfirm.com

CONTENTS

INTRODUCTION

Creating a business can be one of the most rewarding experiences in an entrepreneur's life. It is exhilarating, risk-bearing, roller-coaster riding, "oh my Goodness, what have I gotten myself into," kind of fun. Building a small business can also be daunting and scary. Sometimes we need the money, to pay bills, live, and eat something other than ramen. Sometimes we don't have the know how to get the business up and running.

There are many great resources for starting a business, and if you know where to look, you can find something or someone who can help you with your goals. But as I started a small law firm with my husband, immediately after graduating law school and passing the bar, I found that there are no real straightforward answers to the plethora of questions we had. I searched high and low and tried, unsuccessfully, to find a succinct and clear cut checklist of tasks and ideas that would be helpful to my business. Many nights we didn't sleep trying to piece together ideas and make sure our plan was sound. I decided, that if I could finally piece together all the moving parts and components and start my own successful start-up, that I should try to help others with their business dreams and write up a checklist for starting a small business.

Hence this micro-book. I am writing this checklist, not to be exhaustive, but to be a list that small business entrepreneurs, who are trying to start up or have just started out, can use to check off relevant tasks. This checklist is meant to be a brainstorming tool; an entrepreneurial fire igniter of sorts… and if it does not help you with your business, I guess you could use it as an actual fire starter. If it helps even one entrepreneur, one mini tycoon, one capitalist in training to realize his or her business potential, then I will feel like my goal is accomplished. I wish you all the very best of luck.
Now, get to it!

1
THE BUSINESS SKELETON

Step One: Business Plan

First things first. You need a plan. I know I know, how many times you have heard that. But it is true. You need a plan. So, where to begin. Take out a pen and paper, or if you are the electronic type, start composing a draft email to yourself. Either way, start writing down the concept of your business. Compile a word bank that symbolizes your business. For an example, if you are trying to become a new photography company, start with words like "wedding" "bat mitzvah" and "graduation." Keep adding words alone until you have started a narrative for yourself. Then start to compile a more structured plan. Start pondering what you want to be known as. Depending on your business structure, which we will discuss in the next step of this stage, you will want a catchy name, or something that identifies you; you may even choose to do business as your own name. If not, then try to identify what you do in your business name. There is nothing worse than a small business with a name that people still ask "what do you?", or sell for that matter. So, if you are going to be a photography business in the example above, ponder using artful adjectives and a variation of the word "photography" in the name. Use "photos" "photography" "photographer" or some other word, per this example. It is important to conduct a search of your potential name with local small business administrations, the Patent and Trademark Office, and follow it up with a simple google search. You want to make sure you don't step on anyone's toes when naming your business. Another company may not bring a copyright infringement suit or take issue with your same name, if you are not well known in the business arena. But after following this checklist, you are going to be a power player, so we want to make sure we dot all our i's, cross our t's, and cover our…grounds.

Step Two: Business Structure

You got a plan, now what? Well you should get legal. You need to establish an entity for your business. It could be a sole proprietorship, a limited liability company (LLC), or a subchapter s-corporation (s-corp). Of course, I could totally do a plug for The Machin Law Firm, LLC, and tell you to get a lawyer to help you make this decision and even file your paperwork, but if you are a solo or small business, you can probably make a lot of the decisions on your own. Admittedly, if you are going to do something extreme or complicated, then you should certainly consult a lawyer. In step one we discussed a hypothetical photography business, and if you are trying to do something like this on your own, it may be wise to finish reading through this micro-book and other resources and establish your entity for yourself. After all, it always helps small businesses on a budget to save money. Once you decide the structure that works best for your situation, you need to file with the state you have selected and maintain all the legal entity requirements of the state. This micro-book is well, micro, and meant to be more of checklist, so I won't get into the many factors that business owners consider before establishing their legal entity. I will say, if you are a sole proprietorship, remember that all the liability of your business can still impact you personally. For tax purposes, a sole proprietor may decide to obtain an Employer Identification Number (EIN) from the IRS, but it isn't necessary and the sole proprietor can use his or her own social security number (SSN). Another entity that can experience this type of taxation is a single-member LLC, where the business can be taxed as the individual owner. However, other entities should remember that they need to obtain an EIN for tax and accounting purposes. This is easy to accomplish. Simply visit the IRS website and do a search for "EIN", where you will find the link to apply online. While you are on the IRS website, make sure you are making the correct elections for your business structure and for your success. The IRS website provides in depth and thorough information that can help you make these decisions.

Although this checklist item is brief in this micro-book, this step should not be taken for granted. It is important to know that while your business structure is not permanent, and you can take steps to change the entity of your business, it is best to get this right the first time. Do your research, visit local small business associations, and I hate to say it…but maybe talk to your lawyer. The way you structure your business can have tax and other liability implications… so do your research.

Step Three: Place of Business and Point of Contact

Ok, phew, we got through some of the tough stuff and onto the place of business. Finding the best place to conduct your small business will depend on what you want to do. With the reign of social media and online access, for some small businesses, a physical location may not be necessary. If the small business you wish to start is a service based business, this may be more true now than ever. Service oriented businesses, like law practices or business development firms, are turning to P.O. boxes for mailing addresses and working from home. Now, there are many virtual office providers which also offer what I like to call a P.O. Box on steroids, because they come with a mailing address, someone who will keep your mail, a receptionist who stays at the physical location for walk-ins, and a phone number just for your business, which you can enhance further by paying for the calls to be answered and forwarded to your cell phone. What's even better about these offices, is they offer the ability to schedule office use time also, so if you have a client meeting, you can meet them in "your office" which is a physical location. Of course, the drawbacks include not being able to hang up your diplomas or have your own desk setup, but it works to keep costs down for a small business just starting out.

This logic works for goods oriented small business also. It is much cheaper to rent a storage locker and advertise your goods for purchase online, then it is to rent an entire warehouse or retail store front location. Sometimes even mall kiosks can go for many thousand dollars a month. If you start getting the cash flow to do it, then great, do it...but we are talking about starting up a small business on a tight budget, not a flowing budget.

If virtual just isn't for you, and you don't like the idea of not having a daily permanent location, or maybe you have kids or a dog that prevent you from really focusing at home during the day, then consider subleasing an office by renting a single office in an office suite. There are many classified listings which are locally distributed, and online resources to find these spaces.

It may go without saying that you should tour and ask plenty of questions of potential office space locations before signing a lease. Pay close attention to the look and feel of the staff and the setting to make sure it fits your business and with the type of clients you want. Read your lease thoroughly, and negotiate. These negotiations and contracts can be dense, so sometimes you need to hire a lawyer to review and advocate for fairness and your interests. If you are not going to hire a lawyer, my strongest advice for negotiating for yourself is don't be afraid to ask for more than what is being initially offered. You will surprise yourself to find out how many little benefits and extras you can get out of these office space providers simply by asking for it.

2
BUSINESS OPERATIONS

Step Four: Business Management

So, I feel like this section should be straight forward, but you run the risk of ruining your business if you don't have adequate business management… you know, a system for its nuts and bolts. How are you going to handle the money you earn? Who oversees accounting? Who manages your website? How will you track inventory and sales? How will you manage your client database? This part of this micro-book may serve as a reminder that at this stage of your business, you employ a learn-on-the-go strategy. The thing is, every business, including small business, has a different need. In the practice of law, for an example, it gets tough to handle accounting on your own, so for this type of business, it may be best to hire an accountant. Alternatively, in a baked goods business, you may need a way to track and control for freshness and other issues to remain in compliance with your license to sell foods. Each business will have its own need for tracking, databases, and defined roles. If you are solo, typically, you are everything from the CEO to the janitor, but it doesn't have to be this way, nor do I recommend it. Establish relationships with relevant folks that specialize in fields you don't, like my above accountant example, and seek assistance. My mother used to say, if you sit on too many chairs at once, you fall through. Don't be a jack of all trades and a master of none. If you don't take my advice, I understand. It is hard to hand over some of your valuable data and information, and sometimes you fear that the other person won't care about it as much as you do. Sometimes this is true. For those of you who insist on handling the nuts and bolts on your own, read through the next few steps for more brainstorming.

Step Five: Client and Product Management

This step is crucial for small businesses. Do not skimp on client or product management software or databases. Whether this is formulating an in depth excel document, or purchasing database software, you need something to make sure that you are not losing client information or product information. Inventory is crucial no matter which type of small business you are running. For lawyers, there is a barrage of legal practice management software to choose from. For other businesses, there are many options for customer relationship management software out there. Research all the options, and make sure to take advantage of the free trial periods that these companies offer to make sure you like the software. Chat with others in the industry too and not just the software company representatives regarding the software you are trying, because usually unaffiliated users are able to advise you on the more nuanced inconveniences or features of the software. Some of these software providers offer a streamlined integration of billing software and/or tax software to make life even more manageable. The importance of this integration and ease of use is discussed in the next step.

Step Six: Accounting, Taxes and Payroll

This section is tough to condense into a micro-book considering people write long and dense textbooks on the money matters.

Admittedly, while many of us have passions for selling homemade dog treats or pursuing justice and other noble causes, the money is still very important. In fact, some people do it just for the money. Despite your motivation, accounting is typically a business matter that plagues small businesses, especially at first. The age old wisdom to keep your expenses low, rings especially true for small business start-ups. Depending on your business structure, the degree of difficulty in managing your accounting changes. Sole proprietors have this matter the easiest because they can file and track their spending and gains as themselves. Effectively, sole proprietors are treated as individuals for the purposes of accounting and taxes. Single-member LLCs work this way too. But every other business structure requires much more in depth accounting. The IRS has published countless forms and schedules for all different purposes and the Internal Revenue Code is lengthy and can bore you to death. Unless you are apt in taxation, I highly recommend speaking either to an accountant or a tax attorney.

There are things you can do though, that would keep your preparer costs down. Get an accounting or invoicing software. As discussed above, some customer relationship software integrates into these accounting software and you can easily export cash flow information to this integrated program. Once you have a software that can help tabulate your expenses and profits, and even itemize other relevant information, like payroll, your preparer won't be able to charge you ludicrous amounts of money. After all, you are starting or running a small business and don't have the luxury of spending ludicrous amounts of money. You can help alleviate the work load of a preparer, by getting into a routine of integrating your costs and keeping a clear database.

I can't stress enough the importance of keeping expense receipts. If you are running a successful business, there is a chance that you can be audited by the IRS. I recommend at the very least a shoe box for receipts or a filing cabinet with a file for receipts, but if you can manage it, try to get an electronic receipt organizing system. Try to scan and import your receipts into a program that will help you keep track of your expenses and maintain physical proof of the expense. Try to keep your records for three years; this is where an electronic record may be helpful. It is also helpful to maintain electronic records if you do not have endless filing cabinet storage or space, like someone who works from home or a virtual office. Some records are required to be kept for up to seven years for an IRS audit. Talk to your accountant or tax attorney for personalized advice on how long to keep your records.

Another thing to consider under this section is your payroll processing. As a sole proprietor or as a single-member LLC, it is easier to pay yourself, employees, or contractors via checks right out of your operating account (which we will discuss more in the next step), but as any other entity, it is vital to consider a payroll service to help you keep your transactions clean. Accounting is tough, but try to integrate and streamline your books, speak with a professional, and I am confident the money matters do not have to stymie your progress.

Step Seven: Business Credit and Debit Accounts

This may sound elementary, but do yourself a huge favor and get a SEPARATE bank account from your personal account. Something about being a sole proprietor or a single-member LLC has some small business folks thinking it is OK to co-mingle personal and business funds. I hate to break it to you, but it is not OK. You need to have a separate checking account, savings account, credit card, and in some professions, trust accounts, for your business only. This is important for several reasons, but the first one is truly for liability purposes. Some business entrepreneurs think that if the follow step two and get legal, as in, create an LLC or other entity, that this will blanketly protect them from liability. It won't. We will discuss insurance in the next step, but for now, know that co-mingling of funds can effectively wipe away your limited liability protection, if you cannot show clearly in which capacity you are acting from one transaction to the next. What does this mean exactly? Let's try an example. Let's say you are BizDev, LLC and conduct business development alone, as in, you are a single-member LLC. Someone hires you to help them with their website, and pays you $1500 to do so. You deposit your $1500 into your co-mingled bank account, because you did not read this micro-book. Then you pay your cable bill from the same account in the amount of $100. Then you had other bills that get paid out of that account. Then you had another client that paid you for services, which you deposited into the same account. Then you had a business bill you paid out of that account. Then you have another client, etc. etc. etc. If that first client is unhappy with services rendered, or even worse, sues you for the job done, then the first question is how can you account for which funds are which? The second question is how would a court see you behaving; as an employee of BizDev, LLC or as you, an individual? There are many more questions to ask now, but the second question presented here is very, VERY important. If a court decided it was too difficult to tell under which capacity you were acting, as the employee or as yourself, it may find that you were acting as an individual. In that case, your precious limited liability status, just got real cloudy, and you could be personally liable for the damages caused.

One of the best ways you could ever make a case to protect yourself and make clear that you are acting as an employee of your business during any given transaction, is to make sure the funds go into and out of a separate *business* bank account.

Step Eight: Insurance

In a previous life, before I started law school, I was a personal insurance agent with a large insurance company. While I was comfortably familiar with personal insurance products and liability, and this is a business insurance section, a lot of the same lessons I learned still apply here. The fact is, life throws you curveballs. It is infinitely crucial for businesses, especially small businesses, to be fully insured for liability and malpractice (if applicable). The businesswoman in me agrees with those of you who object to paying for expensive liability policies, especially when you don't anticipate that you will do anything wrong. Sometimes even the best intentions can result in bad outcomes. This is why the lawyer in me makes me write this step of this micro book. It is nearly impossible to account for all possible missteps in conducting business. If you are providing products which get manufactured by a third party this may be increasingly true. Whenever we are a providing a product or a service to a client, we are opening the doors to our own liability and our business liability. This is why we need insurance.

For most small businesses, premises liability is sufficient to cover any accidents, injuries, or other business related incidents which result in a liability to a client or other person. For others, we also need malpractice insurance, like for realtors, insurers, lawyers, doctors etc. It is important to note that some of these professionals need both insurances: premises insurance and malpractice insurance. To understand what each insurance does is relatively simple. Premises liability policies cover incidents that occur on your business premises. So for an example, if someone slipped and fell in your new bakery, this insurance would kick in to cover any liability you may have for the customer's fall. Sometimes you may not have been liable, but this insurance also covers your legal representation in these matters. Since you cannot control if someone wanted to bring a suit against your new bake shop, it is crucial you have this insurance to protect yourself. Even if you plan on working from home, if you meet a client or a customer at your house, and they suffer an injury or loss of some kind, this act would need business premises liability insurance to cover it because a personal home or renter's policy will not. Virtual office space users may also need premises liability for any potential coffee spills, trips, or falls that a client or customer may have while in your virtual office. The companies providing the virtual office space to you have insurance for *your* liability but *not* for your client's liability; that's your job to have.

So then what is malpractice insurance? Malpractice insurance is insurance which protects certain professionals from errors done while rendering their services to clients, customers, or patients. Again, you may not have committed an error, but if a recipient of your service sues you, it is crucial to have this insurance to defend yourself from the suit. Effectively the question you need to ask is, at the time of a lawsuit or an incident of liability, who do you want to have the deep pockets, your insurance company or yourself vis-a-vis your business? Most small business folks will answer that they want their insurance company to cover these issues, but then don't carry adequate insurance, or even worse, none at all.

While it may not be entirely related for all small business owners, it may be more relevant for sole proprietors and single-member LLC owners to note, that it could also be wise to consider maintaining a personal liability policy as well to ensure personal liability protection in the event you get named individually for an issue in a lawsuit.

Insurance costs money, and it is understandably frustrating for a small business owner to have to dish out hundreds if not thousands of dollars on it. But think, in the long run piece of mind is everything and it could cost way more to defend a lawsuit or worse, pay out a claim out of the business's or your own pocket. Get multiple quotes with multiple companies and price compare. It is very easy to change companies also. Speak with an agent and get properly insured.

3
MARKETING AND GROWTH

Step Nine: Website and Social Media

The third element in this checklist is marketing. This is my favorite part. Marketing is a business's lifeline. Without marketing, a business can hardly get clients. Without clients, a business can hardly make money. Without money, a business can hardly survive. Marketing is fun, important, and usually expensive…but it doesn't have to be. This section is one of the biggest motivations for this micro book. I really wanted to help small businesses understand that there are many cool ways to cut costs on marketing, without cutting the effectiveness of marketing. If we all had the money for the most amazing front page ads, or TV segments, or branded schwag, we would do it all! Right? Right. But usually, a small business doesn't have an endless marketing budget, it's a small business after all. While all of the ideas outlined here do require capital and a budget, this section is meant to help keep some of these costs down in innovative ways and still get the word out there.

The first step to good marketing, is to build and maintain a website.

In this day and age, a business without a website, is like a fishing line without a hook… you aren't going to catch anything, or in this case, anyone. A website legitimizes the status of your business and allows potential clients and current clients to familiarize themselves with your products or services. One of the first things a potential client does when they come across you or your business, is check out your website. Unfortunately, website development costs some serious money and if you have contacted a professional website developer, they usually want several hundred or even thousands of dollars. It's typically several hundred dollars for a more basic website, where as if you need more bells and whistles the cost goes up.

Typically, if you are a small business, a more basic website is very suitable. If you are sticking to the basics, you can cut some serious website development costs by doing a lot of it yourself. First, you need a domain. A domain is a URL that is specific for your website. I recommend trying to use a URL that comports with your business name. For example, if you are named XYZ Bake Shop, try xyzbakeshop.com as a domain. If your domain is taken or very expensive, try variations of your business name for your domain. Consider using .net or .biz as necessary, but try to avoid these domain types. Dot coms are usually superior, so try your best to get a .com. There are many companies that offer domains for cheap. Try to do a search for discounts, coupons, or promotions and sometimes you can get your domain for as low as 99 cents. If you don't have a separate business address or phone number, my recommendation is that you get a private registration for your domain. This helps keep that information private and protected so that your home address and phone number don't get sold to marketers or other third parties.

Next, you'll need to get a website development software. Do your research here. Pick a program that suits your capability and comfortability with building your website. For several dollars a month, you can get a streamlined plug and play type website development program, sometimes even through the company that you buy your domain from. Some of these website programs also provide technical support free of charge included with your purchase of their website development program. From here, you plug in your information and start developing your website.

If the idea of creating your website by yourself doesn't make you feel comfortable, then you can get help from online providers in building your website. Try to cut costs here by having a majority of your content already written up. No one knows your business better than you. Write up your motto, your mission, and your product or services information, and this can help cut your costs with a developer. Consider reaching out to local universities or schools and hire an intern to develop the website. College kids are typically happy to get a few extra bucks and are usually able to figure these things out.

This approach may not work for everyone or for all business types, but again, this is just meant to be a brainstorming tool for small or start-up businesses. While we are discussing websites, it is important to remember that a social media page is also very important for a small business. Social media is crucial to modern day marketing. Make a business Facebook page, LinkedIn page, and maybe even Instagram or Twitter, as appropriate. Post sparingly and wisely. Remember, this is your business page. Consider leaving the politics, religion, opinions, and other personal stuff for your other pages, and avoid these issues on your business page. This advice is only relevant of course if you are not in a small business surrounded around one of these topics. On your business social media pages, post business accolades, events, and information. This is a great way for a small business to post product images, community events' information, coupons, and other relevant business promotion. Make your profile picture a professional image of you, your partners, and/or your business location, and make your cover photo your logo. You can configure these images how you like but again, keep it strictly professional. Post your business address, telephone number, work hours and website information. Play around with the configurations of each of these platforms to ensure that you have all of the relevant necessary information for a consumer to get as many questions answered through these pages as they can.

Once you have a website and social media pages, consider doing some search engine optimization or SEO for your pages. On many of these website development programs you can buy an add-on service to conduct SEO for you, or you can add keywords to your website to make sure your website starts to show up in Google searches. Start asking friends and family to visit your website and follow your social media pages; the more the merrier. This will help your business reach more people. Another way to reach people is to use your website and your social media pages to get contact information for potential clients and then follow up with them via these pages or via an electronic or mail newsletters. Remember, your website and your social media pages are in the aggregate the online face of your business. In this day and age, it is more important than ever to make these pages professional and maintain them regularly.

Step Ten: Business Cards and Schwag

Along with the rest of your online marketing, you need physical marketing reinforcements also. The best thing for this, is business cards. Business cards, like all other marketing items, require an artistic touch. Typically, small business owners use their logos to help bring this creative element to the business cards and schwag. If you are able to create your own logo, more power to you. If you have no idea where to start with your logo, you can hire a logo expert or even better, get a few quotes from online programs which can create a logo for you. For a hundred dollars or less, you can get a decent logo created for you, using your colors of choice and language of choice. Use this logo on all of your marketing items. For your business cards, make sure you include your business address, phone numbers, fax number, as necessary, website, and email address. Sometimes, a professional headshot is also an elegant addition to business cards, and helps folks remember you. You can buy templates and the cardstock and print your business cards yourself. Otherwise, there are many business card printing services, where you can upload your logo, use your colors, add your information, and easily have them shipped to you for a reasonable cost. Consider searching for coupons and discount codes for these services. If you are going to order cards, or even print them yourself, try a smaller number of cards to start. I recommend 100 or less. This gives you the opportunity to hold the cards, feel them and see them completed, before wasting resources on too many cards.

This same logic applies to other marketing schwag. As will be discussed in the next step, community events are a great way to get your name out there. If you are going to attend these events and represent your business, you will need schwag. Even if community events are not in the cards for you, it is important to have some marketing schwag. Invest in some branded pens, notepads, hats, bags, mugs etc. Do your research. There are many companies online and locally that can provide these items for you, so do your price comparison. Please note that some of these companies have some product minimums, so try to call and negotiate for them to send you free samples first. Once you get some good clients or customers, it is always nice to provide them with a some free schwag, which just happens to be branded with your business name and logo, and does some free marketing for you as they use the items!

Step Eleven: Community Events

As mentioned in Step Ten, setting up a booth at community events is one of the best ways to get your business name out in your community. I have had some of best success and best clients when I attended community events. It is a great way for your community to *come to you*. There is no worse kind of marketing than the pushy, "overwhelm and bully your potential client into buying your product or service" type marketing. Sometimes a small or start-up business strapped for cash may resort to this type of guerilla marketing. Attending a community event is a way to calm it down and allow potential clients to come to you. They approach your booth as they find it necessary and sign up for your email list voluntarily. These people who walk up to you and sign up with their contact information for your follow up, are the most willing potential clients you can ever find, and are potential clients who *want* to do business with you. These events also give you a chance to present and sell, not only your products or services, but yourself. We all wish to have the most innovative product or service, but sometimes we are in a profession that is dime a dozen. Depends on where you are located, some lawyers, realtors, insurance agents, doctors, and farmers know exactly what I am talking about. If the market is saturated with professionals ready and able to provide your particular product or service, then your marketing should focus on what differentiates you and what makes you better than the rest. Community event marketing is the best way to do this: to sell yourself, to your most willing potential clients.

There is many ways to effectively market via community events. Some best practices include having a contact information sign-up sheets, have candy or balloons, and stand in front of your table. Never hide in the back of your booth. Try to be mobile and invite people into your booth. For product based businesses, set up a few star products at the front and some in the rear, fill in your less favorite products in the middle. Do not over fill the space. Try to leave some breathing room in between your products. If you are selling product on site, make sure you have enough to keep your booth populated. Another thing to remember is to sell products priced for the nature of the community event. Don't come to a fun, daytime, Fall event trying to sell investment grade pearls. Try to temper your products or services to the nature of the community event that you are marketing at.

Before taking on the task of marketing at a community events, try attending some, as a potential client or customer, first. This will help give you an alternative perspective, a chance to see the techniques of other small businesses, and the ability to judge for yourself what works well in your community and what just doesn't. I do highly recommend getting involved in this way, if you want to earn your community's business.

Step Twelve: Maintenance

All of these steps, as discussed, may appear as a one-time effort. And some of them are. However, most of these steps are meant to be maintained and continued. Your website, your schwag, your social media pages, and community events are all examples of steps that require a continuous effort that you need to make on a regular basis. Create a schedule to make sure you don't forget to post to your social media pages, update your website with new relevant information, do some more search engine optimization, and register for events. Dedicate some time every morning to blog or write on your social media pages, post a picture of your previous day's work, or start a new promotion. Keep your business fresh in the mind of your potential clients.

It is also important to keep your books up to date, your management software working, and inventory in check. Maintenance of your efforts thus far is crucial to ensuring continued success. If you have collected a lot of client information, consider maintaining your relationships by newsletters, holiday cards, and other outreach efforts. In the beginning, when a new small business is most exciting, it is easy to remember that customer service is your first goal. As time goes on, and as success starts to pour in, it is easy for small business owners to get complacent or focus merely on their bottom line. Never forget the strategies and efforts that it took to get you to this stage. Instead, maintain these efforts, marketing, community events, and feel for customer service.

4
CONCLUSION

Running a small business can be one of the most awarding experiences in life. While this step by step checklist is not exhaustive, it is a great tool to use to help keep focused and provide some brainstorming direction to folks in early stages of their business or even when just starting out. Each business strategy or decision should be tailored to the business. Just remember to reach out to others in the industry, make connections, and do good business. As long as you act with integrity and value true customer service, your small business is destined to succeed! Remember to find innovative ways to cut costs, maintain your marketing efforts, and keep at it. The English theologian and historian Thomas Fuller once wrote that "the darkest hour is just before the dawn." This sentiment is especially true in running a small business. Things may seem to sour before they succeed, but stay focused and keep your determination!

Good luck!

ABOUT THE AUTHOR

Attorney Rada A. Machin is an experienced small business entrepreneur. Mrs. Machin's office is located in Rockville, MD and she is a Founding Partner and Owner of The Machin Law Firm, LLC. Mrs. Machin started her boutique law firm alongside her husband Manuel D. Machin.

Mrs. Machin is a proud member of the Maryland State Bar Association, the Bar Association for Montgomery County, Maryland, the American Bar Association, the Maryland Association for Justice, and the Maryland Criminal Defense Attorney's Association.

Mrs. Machin went to law school with her husband at the University of the District of Columbia-David A. Clarke School of Law, where she earned her Juris Doctorate and graduated *cum laude*. Mrs. Machin is a Georgetown University Alumna, where she graduated with a Bachelors of Arts in Government and Portuguese.

Mrs. Machin is passionate about her work and is committed to aiding small businesses develop and grow.